THIS BOOK BELONGS TO:

_____

_____

Free Bonus Gift Giveaway!!

Sign up on explorearthursworld.com to receive your gift!

ISBN: 978-1-950904-07-5 (Paperback)
ISBN: 978-1-950904-08-2 (Hardcover)
Library of Congress Control Number: TXu002163604
Edited by Jennifer Rees
Cover design and Illustrations by Judith San Nicolás (JudithSDesign&Creativity)
Edited by Jennifer Rees

SOLAR SYSTEM
AMAZING
SPACE ADVENTURE

GENE LIPEN

He packed up his luggage, amazement in sight,
Arthur's adventure is about to take flight.
Let's wish him the best on his journey and state:
"We are ready to fly,
The Solar System awaits!"

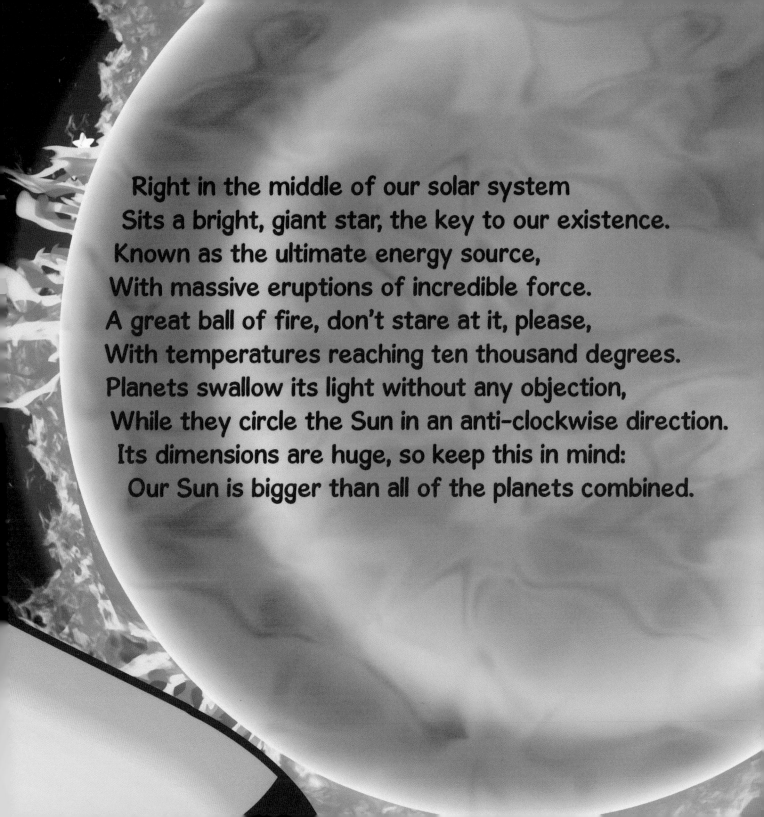

Right in the middle of our solar system
Sits a bright, giant star, the key to our existence.
Known as the ultimate energy source,
With massive eruptions of incredible force.
A great ball of fire, don't stare at it, please,
With temperatures reaching ten thousand degrees.
Planets swallow its light without any objection,
While they circle the Sun in an anti-clockwise direction.
Its dimensions are huge, so keep this in mind:
Our Sun is bigger than all of the planets combined.

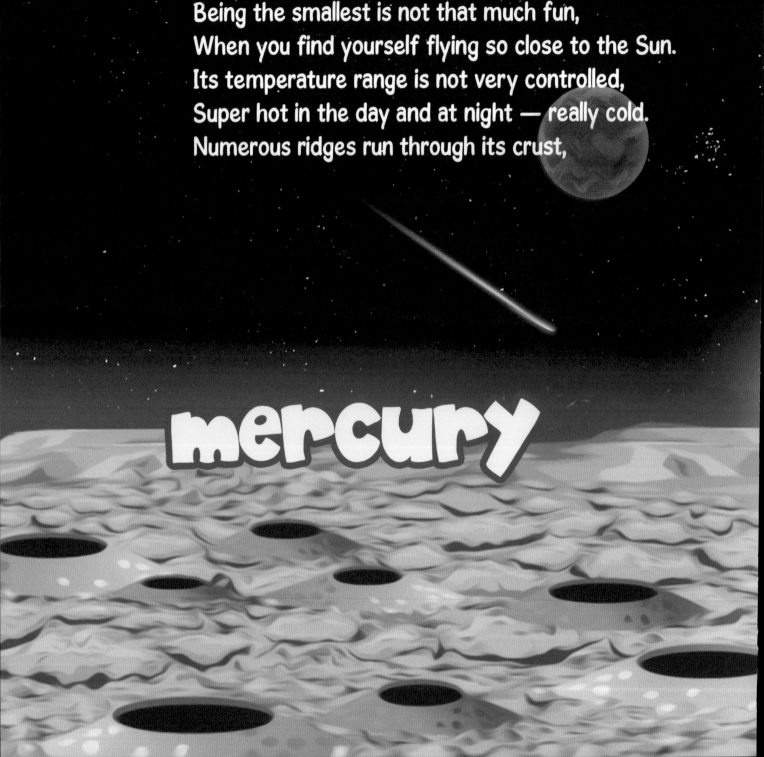

Being the smallest is not that much fun,
When you find yourself flying so close to the Sun.
Its temperature range is not very controlled,
Super hot in the day and at night — really cold.
Numerous ridges run through its crust,

mercury

Covered in thick, dark gray layers of dust.
It is full of sizable craters all over the surface,
And rocks lay around without any purpose.
What is lacking in size, it makes up in speed:
Mercury's flight is the fastest indeed.

Covered by clouds and hidden from view,
Venus looks like a perfect white circle of goo.
Hotter than all other planets by far,
It shines in the sky like a bright little star.

Dry like a desert, the wind terrorizes,
Full of volcanoes and rocks of all sizes.
Visiting Venus is a difficult mission
Due to the horrible surface conditions.

It is third from the Sun and very well known,
Earth is the name, but we call it home.
Perfectly filled with abundance of life,
And ideal conditions where animals thrive.

Warm at the equator and cold at each pole,
Rivers, forests, and oceans make this planet whole.
It never gets lonely throughout day and night,
With its constant companion, Moon, in its sight.
Earth is the liveliest planet by far —
We should never forget just how lucky we are.

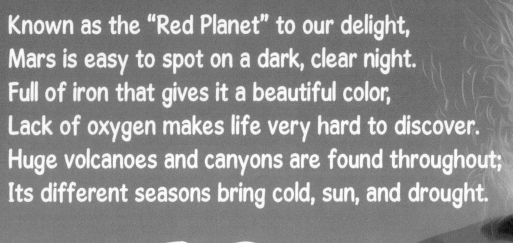

Known as the "Red Planet" to our delight,
Mars is easy to spot on a dark, clear night.
Full of iron that gives it a beautiful color,
Lack of oxygen makes life very hard to discover.
Huge volcanoes and canyons are found throughout;
Its different seasons bring cold, sun, and drought.

Martian gravity will make you feel tall —
You could jump three times higher, no problem at all.
Bring your warm clothes, if you don't want to freeze,
Mars' temperature averages minus 80 degrees.

Covered in stripes and with weather defiant,
Wind is the king on this gas supergiant.
Colossal dimensions help it control
Over 70 moons that keep constant patrol.

jupiter

Largest of all, but here is a surprise:
It spins faster than planets much smaller in size.
Jupiter's color is frequently changing,
Due to huge storms, which are consistently raging.

Named the fabulous "jewel" of our solar system,
For Saturn's colorful rings, it's so hard to resist 'em.
Moving in perfectly circular patterns, they must,
Filled with pieces of ice, parts of rocks, and fine dust.

Saturn

Surface particle sizes are not very aligned,
Some are as tall as huge buildings, and some you can't find.
Standing on Saturn is an impossible task,
Since mostly it's made of helium gas.
Grab your telescope and enjoy a great sight —
Viewing Saturn at night is a tiny delight.

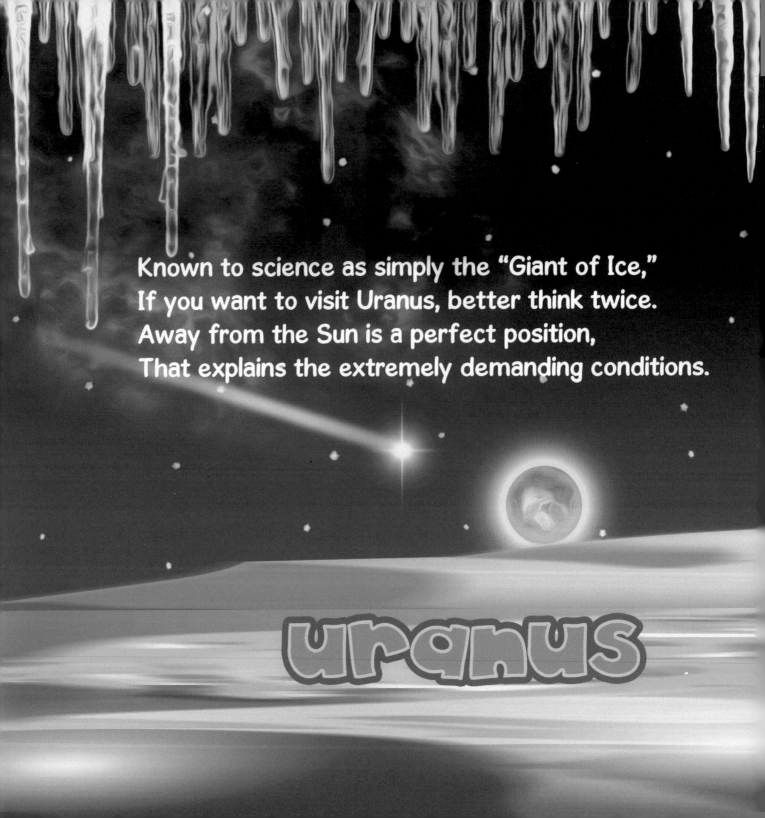

Known to science as simply the "Giant of Ice,"
If you want to visit Uranus, better think twice.
Away from the Sun is a perfect position,
That explains the extremely demanding conditions.

uranus

It looks like the laziest planet you can find,
Since it orbits the Sun while lying on its side.
A mixture of gases make the colors look prime,
Like a pale cyan disk that is frozen in time.

Farthest away from the warmth of the Sun,
Neptune's violent weather will make you pack and run.
Freezing, mind-blowing winds leave one chilled to the bone,
They are 10 times more powerful than Earth's ever known.

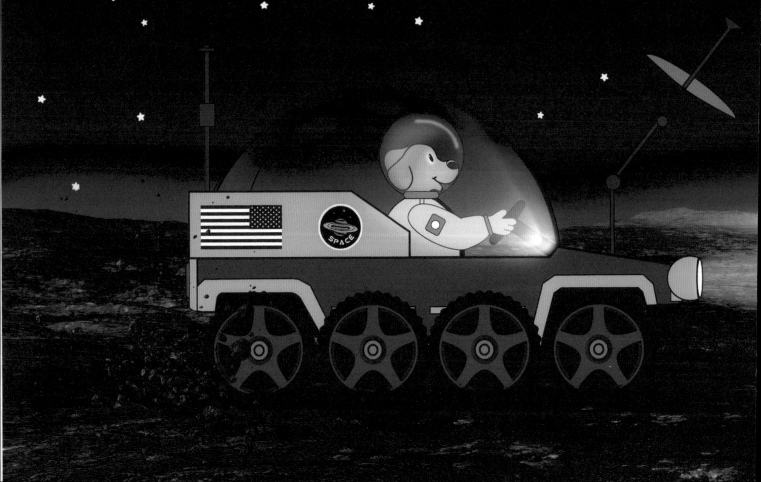

60 thousand days of slow and steady advance
Is what Neptune needs to circle the Sun even once.
Finding this planet is tough in the sky —
You won't be able to see it with your naked eye.
Telescope is a must if you want to set your sights
On its lively blue color, shining clear and bright.

Thank you for joining our outer space flight,
Throughout the vast solar system, with all of its might.
This story is ending, but we all can assume,
Another Arthur adventure will be coming soon!

Thank you for reading. If you enjoyed this book, please consider leaving an honest review at your favorite store.

Check out more books about Arthur in the Kids Books For Young Explorers series

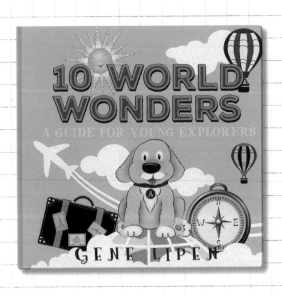

fun coloring pages

enjoy!

I LIKE THIS BOOK, BECAUSE:

_____

_____

Printed in Great Britain
by Amazon